HERTFORDSHIRE
IN OLD PHOTOGRAPHS

DAVE RANDLE

FROM THE JUDGES POSTCARD ARCHIVE COLLECTION

SUTTON PUBLISHING

Sutton Publishing Limited
Phoenix Mill · Thrupp · Stroud
Gloucestershire · GL5 2BU

First published 2003

British Library Cataloguing in Publication Data
A catalogue record for this book is available from
the British Library.

ISBN 0-7509-3385-2

Typeset in 11/13.5 Sabon.
Typesetting and origination by
Sutton Publishing Limited.
Printed and bound in England by
J.H. Haynes & Co. Ltd, Sparkford.

Introduction

In the heart of the country and flowing with life-giving watercourses such as the Colney, the Stort, the Ver and the Hiz, the meadows and gently wooded slopes of Hertfordshire have attracted settlers since the dawn of time. Iron Age Man built fortresses here and established England's oldest trunk route, the Ridgeway, over five thousand years ago.

During the first century BC Celtic communities developed and the pattern of routes and settlements began to take shape, so that by the time the Romans arrived in the first century AD they were able to build on existing infrastructures.

Their major centre in Hertfordshire was Verulamium – present day St Albans. Founded in AD50, it persisted as one of the most important Roman cities in Britain for four hundred years. Standing right on Watling Street, the main cross-country route from their point of entry on the East Kent coast, Verulamium came also to be known as Watlingchester before it took on the name of England's first Christian martyr, St Alban, in the late eighth century.

As elsewhere in the realm, it took the towns and villages some time to 'get over' the Roman occupation. The framing of their own laws and systems to replace those imposed on them by the conquerors did not happen overnight. And, in the meantime, centuries of resentment led to everything Roman, good or bad, being rejected out of hand. Gradually, however, the people settled back into normality.

The next characters to enter stage left were the Normans. We hear plenty about Battle, Hastings and poor old Harold's eye. Undoubtedly William's victory on the edge of the Sussex downs was the turning point. But the actual transfer of power from the Saxon to the Norman kings took place in Berkhamsted. It will come as a surprise to many people that Berkhamsted was also the site of the first Norman castle in England.

Once again, for the most part, the Normans didn't build new towns and cities. They took over the running of existing ones, though they often changed the emphasis, as from the Saxon settlement now known as Northchurch to the new Norman church at Berkhamsted.

Before long just about everywhere had its own Norman church, built in the singular Hertfordshire style. During this time many of the county's fine houses, abbeys and monasteries were also built.

Hertfordshire provided the stage for all sorts of royal goings on, from the imprisonment of King John to that of Elizabeth I. The first Battle of St Albans in 1455 opened the War of the Roses with a victory to the Yorkist forces of the Duke of Warwick and the second, six years later, ended in victory for the Lancastrians of Queen Margaret.

In more peaceful times the county has been the scene of some of the great achievements of the industrial age. The Grand Union Canal opened up trade between London and the North and many of the towns of Hertfordshire benefited from being on its path. Many still do, although the industrial significance of the canals is no more. The legacy of the navigators lives on in fine parklands, locks, towpath walks and the huge leisure potential of these tranquil watercourses.

The railway had a still greater effect, transforming a convenient country retreat of the comfortably-off into a commuter-belt for those whose daily presence in the capital was necessitous but less than desirable. Suddenly the city was only an hour away from the kind of countryside towns everyone dreamed of living in.

The inevitable result of this was that more and more people wanted to move to the county and the demand resulted in a building boom. Soon there were fears that so many Londoners were moving out that London and Herts would join in the middle. So the so-called green belt was set up to protect the countryside and supply a natural buffer between the capital and the expanding towns to the north.

The need for this buffer was made more vital by the fashion for 'new towns'. Hertfordshire occupies a unique position in the history of this phenomenon. Letchworth, Hatfield, Welwyn Garden City – these are just some examples of more or less successful applications of the idea of conceiving and planning an entire town. Unlike the traditional organic growth from medieval streets to traffic-jammed conundrum, trapped by its own history, these places were laid out by people of vision with one eye on the future.

Also unlike the organically grown old towns, they are not always now seen as things of beauty, but few would argue that they are completely without success in what they set out to achieve. They are, for the most part, user friendly – and they have facilities that simply could not be accommodated in the old towns without committing the sin of demolition.

Most are suffering from the universal surfeit of motor vehicles that gives all town planners everywhere a headache. At the same time they seem less prone to the public transport shortcomings that exacerbate this problem elsewhere. The new towns had buses and trains 'designed in'.

And nowadays it is neither the canals nor the railways that determine the fortunes of a town or county. The M25, the A1M, the M1, the A41 and the M11 are the major influences on the Hertfordshire landscape in the early years of the new millennium. And, like all the influences before them, they will leave a mark and they will change the way people live.

But history tells us that one day they will slip peacefully into the past, like Verulamium, the Welgar Shredded Wheat factory and the Grand Union Canal.

This first selection from the Judges Postcards archive recalls more tranquil times. Some images are nostalgic; others reveal a forgotten time when our grandparents travelled these same roads.

Most of these pictures have not been seen for a very long time, so it is hoped that they will bring pleasure and new understanding to the people of Hertfordshire themselves, as well as to visitors, historians and anyone interested in the changing face of human life.

HERTFORDSHIRE
IN OLD PHOTOGRAPHS

Aldbury, nestling at the foot of the Chilterns, is everyone's vision of a traditional English village, with its stocks, pond and whipping post. Only the telegraph poles and TV aerials date this unchanging scene to the 1960s.

Another view of the pond at Aldbury. Tasmanian-born novelist Mrs Humphry Ward made her home at the nearby Stocks House. Possessed of a highly developed social conscience for her time, she was responsible for a number of schemes for the betterment of conditions, including founding the Invalid Children's School in 1891. She is buried in Aldbury churchyard.

The parish church of St John the Baptist at Aldbury enjoyed a renaissance during the industrial revolution, thanks to the patronage of canal baron the Duke of Bridgewater. But by the latter half of the twentieth century it had settled down with its memories, much as we find it today.

Like the moated houses of the past, canals have become very much a feature of the Hertfordshire countryside, providing a peaceful contrast to the bustling nature of the towns and motorways. What was once an industrial thoroughfare has provided rest and recreation for the people of Berkhamsted for generations.

Ashlyns School at Berkhamsted, strangely quiet here in the mid-1960s, was actually established as a hospital for foundlings.

Now owned by the National Trust, the Ashridge Estate covers much of the land around Berkhamsted, Tring and Aldbury. This monument to the Duke of Bridgewater dates from 1832.

These four views of Berkhamsted's High Street in the 1960s clearly demonstrate how much the pace of life has increased in the last forty years. Although a good deal of building has gone on since then, most of the town's citizens still live within a half mile of this road.

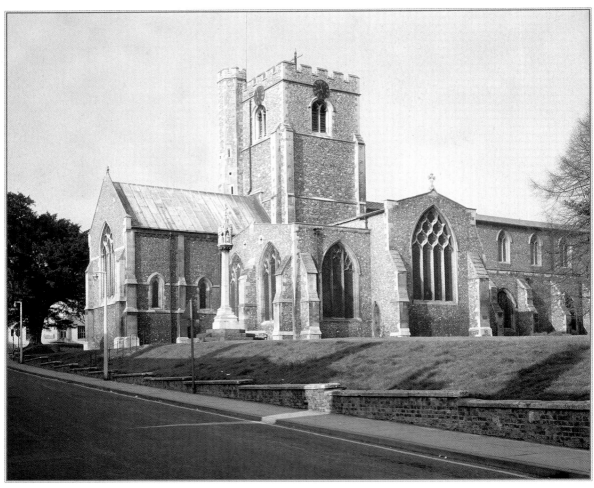

St Peter's church at Berkhamsted was founded by the Normans, but suffered the ravages of uneven fortune through later centuries before being restored in the late nineteenth century.

Its significance to the conquerors whose victory on the battlefields of Sussex had been officially ratified in Berkhamsted is evident in its scale and the fact that it is a prototype of what would become known, many centuries later, as the Early English style of church architecture.

Still preserving much of its ancient character, Northchurch probably got its name when the Normans built what is now St Peter's church at Berkhamsted.

Opposite: It is rare to see two pictures from different eras with as few changes as these. Tree growth would suggest that the bottom picture is the older, but this is clearly not the case. It is more likely that this picture was taken during the winter months. The cars date it to the 1960s, where the earlier picture has no cars at all. Apart from the replacement gate, the Boote Inn seems completely unchanged.

St Mary's at Northchurch had been a place of worship for the Saxons for the best part of two centuries before the building of St Peter's.

Berkhamsted's was the first Norman castle in England, commissioned by William the Conqueror's brother, Sir Mortain, following the passing of the throne to William in the town in 1066. The original wooden keep was destroyed in 1104, but its stone replacement had a career spanning the next four hundred years, including a spell as the residence of Thomas Becket, and another as a prison for King John of France, following his capture in the Battle of Poitiers in 1356.

Dean Incent's House in Berkhamsted High Street was built in the late fifteenth century, when the Duchess of York resided at Berkhamsted Castle and the Dean was her secretary. It is believed to have been the birthplace of his son, John, who would become Dean of St Paul's and found Berkhamsted School.

Berkhamsted school has been in existence since the sixteenth century, although its development into one of the 'good' schools really took place over the last two hundred years. Graham Greene's father was headmaster there for a time. It is now Berkhamstead Collegiate School. This picture dates from the mid-1960s.

The Tudor courthouse at Berkhamsted originally had a further overhanging storey, though it had long gone by the time of this 1950s shot.

More nostalgic 1960s images of Berkhamsted High Street. A long-established Roman
road at the time of the Conquest, it remained one of the country's most vital
thoroughfares until the new A41 bypassed the town, and hostelries such as the King's
Arms stand as a testament to its importance.

The wide valley in which Berkhamsted is situated presented itself to the nineteenth-century engineers as the ideal route for the Grand Union Canal. In recent times their superannuated masterpiece has found a new lease of life as a waterborne haven for those in no hurry. The picture above, like those opposite, recaptures the time when canal cruising was about to reach a peak of popularity with the 1964 release of the film *The Bargee*, starring *Steptoe and Son*'s Harry H. Corbett. The building next to the barge in the photograph opposite is now the Crystal Palace pub.

These views of North Street in Bishops Stortford are both taken from Louis Vulliamy's Corn Exchange building. The top picture shows a market in full swing outside the George in the mid-1960s. In the lower picture we're into the 1970s. K-Shoes have adopted a new logo and must have been fed up with getting the wrong mail, judging by the bold new shop number. The intervening years have also seen the arrival of double yellow lines, though they don't seem to have had much effect on parking.

Hertfordshire

In its position directly opposite St Michael's church in Wind Hill, the Boar's Head has played a significant part in the life of Bishops Stortford since the fifteenth century. It retains much of its original character in these 1970s images, though it was remodelled at various times in its long history and its original fifteenth-century entrance was long ago filled in.

29

Formerly known as Hockerill College, Bishops Stortford Boys' College is another of the county's grant-maintained schools, serving both day pupils and boarders from the UK and abroad.

Founder of Rhodesia Cecil Rhodes was born at Netteswell House in Bishops Stortford in 1853. In 1938 the house was turned into a Rhodes Museum and now contains, in addition to a fine collection of African artefacts, an evocative display of Bishops Stortford in the nineteenth century.

Beautifully situated at the top of Wind Hill, the elegant church of St Michael looks down on the ford in the River Stort that gave Bishops Stortford its name.

This sunset image from the 1960s accentuates the unmistakable silhouette of its 180-foot-high spire.

Opposite: Built in the fifteenth century – its construction almost certainly supervised from the Boar's Head opposite – St Michael's probably occupies the site of earlier Saxon and Norman churches.

The unchanging face of St Augustine's parish church in Broxbourne, photographed here in the early 1970s.

The very model of an ideal suburban housing estate; Barnet's Hadley Wood in the 1960s. This is a view along leafy Lancaster Avenue.

Variously known as Hadley Common or Hadley Green, this shows a stately and almost rural side to Barnet, when it was still more 'Herts' than London. In 1471 it was the site of the Battle of Barnet, in which Warwick, known as The Kingmaker, finally met his own end.

Way before Barnet became a London borough in 1965, it had strong associations with the capital. The fair at Chipping Barnet was first held in 1199 and became so well known that it was immortalised in Cockney rhyming slang. This view of the parish church is from Wood Street.

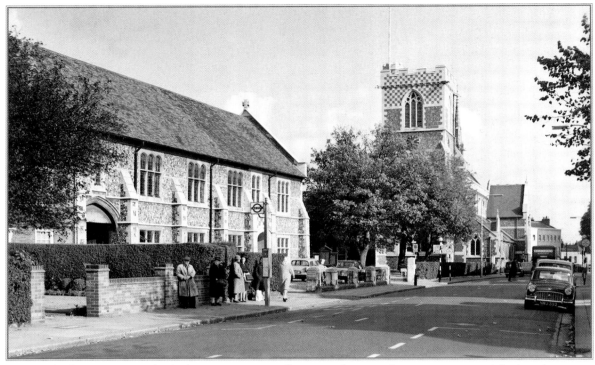

The bus stop outside the historic Ewen Hall in Wood Street close to Barnet parish church.

Opposite: Four postcard views of East Barnet when it was a place to send postcards from. The Isetta bubble car outside Williams Brothers was the latest thing back then – and the only thing in England with the BMW badge on it!

In this picture of Barnet church in the very early 1960s, the trams that once ran this way are no more, but the London bus is a sign of changes to come in a few short years.

EAST BARNET

The Gate at Monken Hadley in the mid-1960s. The first record of Monken Hadley dates from 1489 and its name means the monks' heath or meadow.

Showing a strong stylistic relationship to Barnet's main church, St Mary's at Monken Hadley is seen here in quieter days.

It's fair to say that the county's largest church, St Mary's at Hitchin, has had a chequered history. Built on the site of a Benedictine monastery, founded by King Offa in 792, it was begun in around 1100 on a cruciform pattern with a central tower. In 1115 it was hit by a hurricane, so had to be largely rebuilt. All was relatively calm for the next couple of centuries until the earthquake of 1298, in which the central part of the church collapsed again. Six years later, before the repairs had been completed, the roof fell in. Finally the church elders got the message and moved the tower to the end.

Largely thanks to the various false starts in its construction, Hitchin church has benefited from some of the finest work of fifteenth-century craftsmen, including the famous 'Mousey' Thompson, whose trademark mouse can also be seen in Westminster Abbey, York Minster and churches throughout the land. These two views, taken from Market Place, show the stocky, heavily buttressed tower. No wind or quake is going to knock this baby over. In the forty years or so between the two pictures some new building has gone on beyond the church, but little has changed in the heart of old Hitchin.

Viewed from the other end, Hitchin church would not look out of place in Cambridge. Interesting to see how the willow tree has grown from nothing between the earlier pre-war picture and the one taken in the 1960s.

Idyllic views of Hitchin from Windmill Hill in the 1920s.

This photograph is labelled 'Hitchin, Bancroft, Old Houses'. The description is still truer now, although they've been somewhat prettified and black-and-whited since then. But it even applied back in 1846, when Quaker renaissance man William Ransom founded the pharmaceutical company at Bancroft that still bears his name. He died in 1914, less than ten years before this picture was taken.

Opposite: The heart of Hitchin is laid out in this elevated view in the direction of Market Place taken in around 1970. The building directly behind the parked cars is Gatward's Jewellers. Still there today – and still in the family – it was opened in 1760 in what had previously been an inn for drovers bringing their stock to the market.

The Biggin started life as a monastery on land granted by the Lord of the Manor of
Hitchin in 1361. The building seen here eighty-odd years ago, and still standing today,
was probably built in 1585 by one Robert Snagge, recycling much of the original
structure. The name means a building on a hill. Not a lot of people know that.

With its proximity to London and St Albans and to the ancient northward route that has become the A1, Hitchin has made a good and consistent living from drovers and travellers. As the coaching inns and the market brought wealth to the town, so local trade grew.

The buildings in these views from the 1970s show the uninterrupted economic viability of Hitchin across five centuries.

The Red Hart at Hitchin was one of the first and last staging posts for travellers between London and the north. This view shows the gate by which coaches would enter and leave the yard. No 'lounge' in the inter-war years, note – just a public bar and a 'private' bar.

Although, like every other town in the realm, Hitchin has had to make concessions to
the proliferation of motor transport, the image of Queen Street in the 1920s shows how
generous the width of its ancient thoroughfares has always been. The wide single
pavement here provides plenty of scope for later changes in priorities, and the later
1970s image shows how grace and character could be retained as a result.

Only 17 miles from London, Hoddesdon offered both countryside and convenience to those whose business was in the city. Great Amwell Weir takes its name from one of the two parishes on whose boundaries Hoddesdon is situated. The other is Broxbourne. In the last 150 years both have waned in importance by comparison.

Opposite: Hoddesdon's fortunes through the ages have been dependent on two main factors – the appeal of its surrounding countryside to the well-to-do and its position on the main coach road from London to Cambridge. Both the White Swan and the Old Cock Inn were still thriving in the mid-1960s, though by then group travel was already giving way to the private car and 'coaches by appointment'.

Hoddesdon's Barclay Park preserves a piece of the abundant, rolling, wooded landscape that drew the gentility to this part of the county over the years.

Oakmere Park, Potters Bar, in the early twentieth century. In 1916, not many years before this photograph was taken, the park was the scene of a Zeppelin crash, in which all the crew were lost. Remnants of the airship are on display at the Willyotts Centre in Darkes Lane.

Below: Oakmere House in Potters Bar started life as a gracious Edwardian residence with superb views over the park. In the mid-1990s it was acquired by Whitbread and turned into an eatery. This picture recalls its former tranquillity.

Old meets new in Darkes Lane in the 1960s. The second picture shows the bridge on which the Potters Bar rail crash would occur on 10 May 2002.

This shows part of the medieval manor of Willyotts in Potters Bar. Nowadays there's a restaurant and the Potters Bar Museum.

Long before the arrival of the M25 Potters Bar experienced major expansion in the 1930s, with most of the shops around the railway station and Darkes Lane dating from that time. These High Street pictures from the 1960s still have a 'new town' flavour. However, the expansion was won at the loss of areas of once inviolable 'green belt', unleashing a tide that many are still working to turn. Curiously, the town's name comes from a 'barre' or gate set up to preserve the hunting grounds of a landowner called Potter.

So neat, modern and uncompromising that it looks like a computer-generated graphic, this is Potters Bar's Roman Catholic church in about 1970.

The name of Ivinghoe Beacon recalls the days when braziers were lit on the highest points of the landscape to transmit news and warnings between communities. Fortified and occupied during the Iron Age, it is seen here during the quieter years of the twentieth century, before the Ridgeway, of which it forms part, became a marketing commodity. 'England's oldest road', in use by drovers and travellers for more than five thousand years, currently generates an estimated £800,000 a year for communities along its course.

Sir Robert Lytton bought the original red-brick Tudor mansion at Knebworth in
1490 – five years after he helped Henry Tudor beat Richard III at the Battle of Bosworth
Field to become Henry VII. Knebworth House, as it is known today, is the result of a
transformation undertaken in 1843 by the poetic Edward Bulwer-Lytton, friend to
Dickens, Viceroy of India and Ambassador to France. A frequent visitor was
Sir Winston Churchill, who painted a picture of the banqueting hall seen opposite,
which now hangs there.

Four of the exquisite rooms at Knebworth House. A number of notables added their special skills to the formation of the house as it exists today. Sir Edwin Lutyens married into the family and Gertrude Jekyll designed the herb garden. Nowadays the name of Knebworth is synonymous with the open air rock concerts held in its park.

Hatfield as it is today came into being as a result of the New Towns act of 1946. These pictures taken in the early 1970s capture the success of the grand design, which is still recognised as providing unparalleled facilities and convenience – especially to its student population. The main campus of the University of Hertfordshire dominates the new town. Established in 1951, it specialises in art and design and – appropriate to the home of De Havilland aircraft – engineering. Overall the university has a population of nearly 18,000 students across five campuses, around 1,300 of whom are from abroad.

It's easy to forget that Hatfield existed for centuries before a governmental body enacted it. It originally took the form of 5,000 acres of heath (hence Hetfelle or Heathfield) given by King Edgar in 970 to the monastery at Ely. Royal history was played out here during the doings between Elizabeth and her Catholic half-sister Queen Mary. Elizabeth was held at Hatfield House until Mary's death and delivered her first proclamations in the town's great hall in 1558 on receiving the news. These houses in Broad Oak probably stood then, and are little changed in this photograph from the 1920s.

Opposite: In the manner of brash modern architecture, a number of Hatfield's public buildings of the '50s and '60s – such as the swimming pool and hospital seen here when new – now look as cool and avant-garde as television sets from the same era. At this writing plans for a new hospital are at full wrangle.

Sawbridgeworth is about as far as you can go in the direction of Harlow without being in Essex. Indeed the town itself was part of Essex in the past, but the M11 has marooned it (and Harlow) forever on the Hertfordshire side from now on. This is Great St Mary's parish church.

Two views of Sawbridgeworth in the 1960s, when both the Queen's Head and the Old Bell were starting to push food in a bid to halt the decline in pub-going.

There are no outward signs to indicate what this building at the corner of Sawbridgeworth's High Street and (the already one-way) Bell Street was back in the 1960s. Nowadays it is the Market House pub.

Opposite: Tring in the early 1960s. The town is listed in Domesday as Treunge and appears in the 1199 survey as Trehangr. In either case, the name refers to the wooded slope it occupies on the edge of the Chilterns. Its first major expansion occurred at the end of the eighteenth century with the construction of the Grand Union Canal. A second followed in 1835 when the railway reached Tring with the aid of some major engineering work from George Stephenson, and put the town within an hour of London.

When these pictures were taken Tring High Street was the main road, but was still able to make do with polite 'no waiting' signs. Now the A41 dual-carriageway is supposed to have taken all the traffic, but the High Street is a steeplechase of speed humps.

The Mansion at Tring was built in
1682. Its design is by Sir Christopher
Wren and its first owner was one
Colonel Guy. The house and its park
have passed through various hands
down the centuries, most significant
among these being the Rothschilds.

MP Lionel Rothschild bought the estate at Tring for his son Nathaniel in 1872. He was fascinated with the natural world and established a zoo and museum at the park. He in turn passed the estate to his own son, Lionel Walter, who bequeathed the museum to the nation. The Mansion itself became the Arts Educational School.

As 'Lord of the Manor', Nathaniel Rothschild took his responsibilities seriously. He saw to it that the town had a proper water supply and he commissioned local architect William Huckvale to build new houses in the English vernacular style.

The parish church of St Peter and St Paul, Tring, almost certainly stands on the same site as earlier versions going back to Norman times and beyond. The current building dates mainly from the fifteenth century and is constructed from the characteristic combination of flint and Totternhoe stone to be found elsewhere in the county.

This 1960s shot of the Grand Union at Marsworth near Tring shows a nice mix of serious waterborne business and people just messing about on the water.

A novelty attraction at Tring dating back at least to when this photo was taken in the early 1960s – the famous farm-implement gate.

The great gateway of the monastery at St Albans. St Alban was Britain's first Christian martyr. He was a citizen of the Romano-British town of Verulamium, which occupied the site of what we now know as St Albans from the first to the fifth centuries AD, who lived and was martyred in the third century. The monastery was founded on the site where it was believed Alban's body would have been buried following his execution.

Two views of St Albans
marketplace in the 1980s.
The building now occupied by
Laura Ashley was scheduled for
demolition in 1902. Thankfully
public outcry prevailed.

Ye Old Fighting Cocks in St Albans started out in life as a fishing lodge for the monks from the nearby abbey. Passing to more secular use, it has long held on to its claim to be the oldest inhabited licensed premises in England. Perhaps the most surprising thing about these two images of it, taken many years apart, is the fact that the taller chimney is on the later picture. We are used to seeing ancient chimneys reduced for safety reasons, but here what was a theoretical affair in 1930 has been replaced by a three stage chimney, matching the height of the main flue, in 1965. The reason, of course, has to do with increased pub-grub, new smokeless regulations and the proximity of taller buildings.

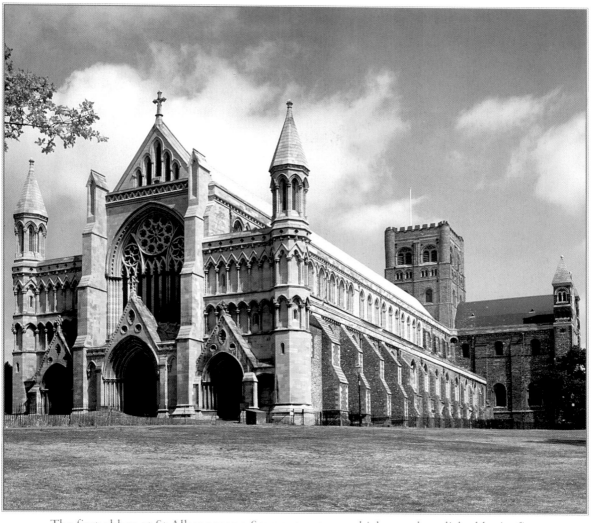

The first abbey at St Albans was a Saxon structure, which was demolished by its first Norman abbot, Paul de Caen, in 1077. He built a new stone one in the Norman style, which lasted until 1539, when Henry VIII had it knocked down during the Dissolution. Then all that remained was the great gate and what had been the abbey church. This became St Albans' parish church. In the thirteenth century it was extended westward until it reached its present length of 550 feet.

This romantic eighteenth-century engraving shows how St Albans church, now a cathedral (since 1877), dominated the skyline, its tower reaching more than 100 feet from its base.

The exquisite symmetry of St Albans Cathedral's decoration is brilliantly displayed in this study by master-photographer John Edwards.

A view of St Albans Cathedral from the north-east in the early part of the twentieth century reveals the presence of a tennis court.

St Albans from the north-west. The storehouse on the left gives the image a French feel with its overgrown roof and sense of organic abandonment.

St Albans from the site of the old Romano-British settlement at Verulamium. One
culture, one civilisation succeeds another.

Two more views of the spectacular interior of St Albans Cathedral – the north aisle and the tower arches. It is believed that the more massy pillars in the transept were recycled from the original Saxon abbey.

Opposite: The Lady Chapel was added to St Albans Cathedral in the fourteenth century. Following the dissolution it became St Albans Grammar School, reverting to its intended ecclesiastical purpose in 1870.

Standing over the shrine to St Alban, the Watching Gallery enabled the monks to keep an eye on pilgrims and the gifts they left behind them. Inside the chamber the martyrdom of Alban is represented in a frieze of solid oak.

St Michael's church stands in the same spot as Verulamium's Roman forum. Built in 948, it retains many of its original Saxon features. A monument to Sir Francis Bacon reminds us that, whether or not he could claim to be Shakespeare, he was recognised in his own time as Viscount St Albans and 'Lord Verulam', forsooth.

The district of St Michael's grew up around a natural fording point on the River Ver. The Romans probably built the first bridge there in about 60AD. Alban himself would have passed across it on the way to his execution. The present bridge dates from 1765, until which time carriages and carts would have continued to use the ford, which itself underwent restoration in 2001. This photograph was taken in the late 1930s.

French Row, St Albans, through the ages. French Row got its name from the French soldiers recruited to help fight King John who were quartered there in 1216. The first image here dates from around 1915 and is a view from behind the famous clock tower. The other two are from broadly similar angles – the first, with Standard 8, from about 1960, and the second, pedestrianised with Laura Ashley, post-1980. None the less certain landmark buildings are clearly identifiable.

The clock tower at St Albans was built in the first decade of the fifteenth century and
restored in the mid-nineteenth by Sir George Gilbert Scott. Looming nearly 80 feet
above the marketplace, it continues to occupy a significant place in the life of the town,
five hundred years on. This view of it from the nearby cloisters was taken just after the
First World War.

As an interesting contrast, this picture was taken from the same archway in the 1970s.

Here's St Albans clock tower in the 1950s – the marketplace one-way even then, but its versatile all-in-one surface ready for anything.

The same spot revisited in the 1980s – pavements and bollards have put an end to all that parking.

An atmospheric view of St Albans in around 1915.

Three views of
St Albans, each
typifying an era. The
Wren porch at Bromley
College retains its air of
the distant past. The
two ladies crossing the
road to the White Hart
Hotel, an ancient
timbered coach house,
could only be doing so
in the 1950s, with or
without the Morris,
whose styling still forms
the basis for the Indian
Hindustan. And the very
sign that proclaims the
building opposite as the
Tudor Tavern places this
view of George Street in
the very recent past.

Cassiobury Park at Watford was originally the grounds of a mansion belonging to the Earls of Essex. The mansion is long gone and the park has become a public place. These pictures from the 1920s show the gatehouse and the Grand Union Canal – which was brought through the park in around 1796.

A lock on the
Grand Union
Canal in Watford's
Cassiobury Park
in the inter-war
years.

The River Gade flowed through Cassiobury Park long before the now-forgotten mansion was built. The park is now the subject of a millennium project that will introduce planned nature trails and a visitor centre.

The Top Rank Watford
Suite in the 1960s was
the place to be. It even
had a 'free off-licence',
which was nothing of
the sort, of course.

Watford Town Hall in the 1960s. Especially fine acoustics have led to the founding of the Colosseum concert venue in recent times. Back in the 1960s composer Laurie Johnson used it as the ideal venue to record his symphony, *Synthesis*. Later, in the film *Hot Millions*, it also doubled as the concert hall in Brazil in which Maggie Smith apparently played the Haydn flute concerto.

Opposite: Watford's Old Free School. There have actually been a number of these over the years from 1575 until education became a national affair in the twentieth century. This one, in Church Passage, was established in 1704.

Another view of Church Passage – a peaceful walkway conceived for pedestrians in a time when transport played little or no part in school and church life.

St Mary's church at Watford has the stocky buttressed tower with the Hertfordshire 'spike' on top, along with the flint infill construction that characterises many of the county's churches.

Two more contrasting views of Watford in the 1960s. Above, another angle on the Top
Rank Suite, looking over the River Colne. It is likely that the town's name comes from
the fact that the Roman Watling Street forded the Colne at this point. And below,
representing the more ancient part of the town, the Alms Houses.

Whatever critics might have had to say about the new towns and garden cities, facilities such as the municipal swimming pools at Welwyn were like nothing previously possible in the organically developed old towns. It's not just the style of the buildings – somehow these pictures could not have been taken at any other time than the 1960s.

Welwyn Garden City was founded by Ebenezer Howard in 1920, though its name will be forever associated in many people's minds with one of the first companies to set up there. Welgar moved to the new location in 1926 and brought the world Shredded Wheat. Although the firm was taken over by the American giant Nabisco in 1938, the product was still branded 'Welgar Shredded Wheat' in the 1960s when these photos were taken.

JUDGES POSTCARDS
A brief history

There is every chance that the postcard you send home from your holiday started life in Sussex. Since 1902 Hastings has been the home of Judges, one of Britain's leading publishers of quality picture postcards.

When Fred Judge arrived in Hastings in 1902 he could have had little idea of the worldwide impact he was to make on the business of postcard publishing. But Fred was a master with a camera and a natural entrepreneur. Fred Judge was born in Yorkshire in 1872. Photography was always his real interest, and it was while visiting Sussex in 1902 that he made the decision to give up engineering for a career as a photographer.

Fred and his brother Thomas purchased an existing business in Hastings and set up as photographers and photographic dealers under the name of Judge's Photo Stores. Although the idea of sending an illustrated card through the post was not new (the first having appeared towards the end of the nineteenth century) Fred made his mark by setting himself extremely high artistic standards. At first he concentrated on local scenes and activities. Having taken his pictures he would go straight back to the darkroom to make them into postcards – often for sale within a few hours; and the quality of his work was such that passers by would gather outside the shop window for a sight of his latest work.

Technically stunning, and using all the latest photographic technology, Fred's pictures won over 100 medals, and one-man exhibitions of his work were held in London, Washington, New York and Tokyo.

Back in Hastings the business was expanding, necessitating moves to bigger and better premises, culminating in the move in 1927 to the purpose-built factory that the company occupies to this day. Although the building has been developed and extended, the Italianate façade remains a famous landmark on the A259 coast road.

Fred Judge died in February 1950 at the age of 78, having built up an internationally respected company. The business was sold to another Judges photographer, who introduced lithographic colour printing. Then in 1984 Judges became a real family concern once again when Bernard and Jan Wolford took over. It became even more of a family business when their son Graeme, now managing director, joined, followed by Trevor, now sales director. The present management can truly be said to be building on the foundations laid by Fred Judge over ninety years ago.

Judges Postcards Ltd, 176 Bexhill Road, St Leonards on Sea,
East Sussex, TN38 8BN
Tel: 01424 420919; Fax: 01424 438538
www.judges.co.uk